W9-ARO-230

Chat... Chat... Chat

by Julie Komorn

SCHOLASTIC INC.
New York Toronto London Auckland Sydney
Mexico City New Delhi Hong Kong

If you purchased this book without a cover, you should be aware that this book is stolen property. It was reported as "unsold and destroyed" to the publisher, and neither the author nor the publisher has received any payment for this "stripped book."

No part of this publication may be reproduced in whole or in part, or stored in a retrieval system, or transmitted in any form or by any means, electronic, mechanical, photocopying, recording, or otherwise, without written permission of the publisher. For information regarding permission, write to Scholastic Inc., Attention: Permissions Department, 555 Broadway, New York, NY 10012.

ISBN 0-439-14772-7
ASCII Art by Christopher Johnson. Glossary researched from Yahoo's Internet Life Surf Lingo.
Copyright © 1999 by Scholastic, Inc. All rights reserved. Published by Scholastic Inc. SCHOLASTIC and associated logos are trademarks and/or registered trademarks of Scholastic Inc.

12 11 10 9 8 7 6 5 4 3 2   9/9 0 1 2 3 4/0
                                                40
Printed in the U.S.A.
First Scholastic Printing, October 1999

Table of Contents

Kidsilly: HF :-)
Friendlee: Hi, WU?
Kidsilly: Playing computer games. WF.
Friendlee: Kewl.
Kidsilly: And u?
Friendlee: Eating 00>
Kidsilly: :9 I'm eating >>>>>=======
Friendlee: :-(*)
Kidsilly: HHOJ
Friendlee: Have you met :] ?
Kidsilly: AFAIK, no. What's his name?
Friendlee: Flurg. He's a FOF's cyber pet.
Kidsilly: OIC. <G> Hi, Flurg! WUF?
Friendlee: He says he's from WWW.
Kidsilly: :D X-I-10
Friendlee: OK, GG (@@)
Kidsilly: IUM. NTYMI, TTG 4 ME 2
Friendlee: CUNS, F2F.
Kidsilly: LD. C-U, Flurg!
Friendlee: KR.

AYK (as you know), there's a whole different way of talking on the internet. It's like a secret code that only 'net users understand. Sometimes this language saves us time. Sometimes it helps us better explain what we mean. And sometimes it's just simply more fun than using regular old English.

Here's a book all about 'net lingo so you can talk the talk — write the write. So go ahead, download these electronic expressions into your mind (i.e., read this book) — and chat it up with your web friends. You may :-) or you may even :-O or :-, but hopefully you will LOL!

Chapter One

SMILEYS

Smileys (sometimes called emoticons) are those little sideways faces that you see sprinkled throughout e-mail messages, instant messages, and chat rooms. Why do we need smileys? To help us communicate. Since we can't hear people's voices in e-mail messages, we can't completely understand the tone or meaning of their statements. Without smileys, our on-line friends could get the wrong impression! Smileys help clarify our on-line conversations. So we can explain to our friends that we are only joking, or that we were just being sarcastic. So, whatever you say, say it sideways — with a smiley.

Smileys are made up of characters typed on a computer keyboard. In addition to expressing emotions, smileys can also convey concepts, activities, animals, caricatures, and other funny stuff. (They're much easier to understand if you tilt your head to the left.)

Here are a few examples:

:-) **This is your basic smiley**. When you add this to the end of your remark, you're explaining that your statement is said with a smile.

;-) **This is a winking smiley**. This smiley is used with a joke. Added to a sentence it says, "This is funny" or "This is supposed to make you laugh."

:-(This is a frowning smiley. This means you did not like that last statement or you are upset about something.

;-(This is a mad smiley. Adding this to a statement shows that you are mad about something.

Example:

Your friend writes: I'm sorry you're feeling sick :-(
You write: That's okay, I'm feeling much better now :-)
But it's a bummer I had to miss b-ball practice ;-(

Here is a complete list of commonly used smileys:

:-)	happy
:-(	sad
;-(	mad
:-I	indifferent
:-))	really happy
>:-(	annoyed
:-{	angry
:-z	angry (variation)
:-{{	very angry
%)	confused
:-/	frustrated
x:-/	uncertain
':-/	skeptical
:0	surprised
8-0	shocked
;-)	winking
:~)	wondering

:-D	laughing
%-D	laughing like crazy
:O	singing
:-9	licking lips
:/)	not amused
(-:	left-handed smiley
:-7	skeptical
:-)~	drooling
:-B	drooling out of both sides of mouth
:-<	frowning
&-I	tearful
:'-(	crying
&.(..	crying really hard
:'-)	crying with happiness
:-V	shouting (variation)
:-@	screaming
:(0)	yelling
:-(O)	yelling even louder
:-#	has braces
:(#)	braces (variation)
`:-)	sweating
,:-)	sweating on other side
I-O	yawning or snoring
I^o	yawning or snoring (variation)
:-`	has a dimple
:-e	disappointed
:-[	pouting
:-}	embarrassed smile

:-S	talking gibberish
:-T	keeping a straight face
:-x	lips are sealed
· :-y	said with a smile
:-Y	quiet aside
:-C	bummed out
~ :-(	really bummed out
#-)	blinking
| :-|	unyielding
:-i	semi-smile
:-j	semi-smile (variation)
:-|	unfazed
;^?	wigged out
~~:-(	getting rained on
O |-)	enjoying the sun
M:-)	saluting
:%)%	has acne
:-!	bored
%-\	tired
%')	very tired
%*@:-(	freaking out
=%-O	stared at computer way too long
:-'|	have a cold
:-))	double chin
:-)))	triple chin
:-)—	thin as a pin
:-,	smirk
;-,	like, duh

:-1	whatever
:-7	wry face
:-8(	condescending stare
:->	sarcastic face
%+{	lost a fight
%-6	all mixed up
%-		been up all night
(:-I	egghead
%-}	dizzy
(:-	blank expression
!#!^*&:-)	total head case

Here's an example of an on-line smiley conversation:

You write: My favorite meal is pizza soup and a large pickle shake. :-9
Your friend writes: 8-O
You write: :-) ~ I love pickle shakes :D
Your friend writes: You're :-S and you're a *!#*!^*&:-)

E-hair

Add some fur to your smiley friends:

):-)	smiley with hair
):-(	frowning smiley with hair
&:-)	curly hair
@:-)	wavy hair
#:-)	messy hair
=:-O	hair standing on end

%-)	long bangs
{:-)	hair parted in the middle
}:-)	hair parted in the middle, sticking up on sides
(-)	needs a haircut
~~:-(	mohawk
~~\8-O	bad-hair day
}(:-(	toupee blowing in wind
:-)}	beard
(:-{~	beard (variation)
:{0	basic mustache
:-{)	mustache (variation)
:-})	handlebar mustache
:-#|	bushy mustache
:-<	pointy mustache
{:-{)}	mustache and beard
)8-)	scuba diver with hair
| :-)	heavy eyebrows
/;-)	heavy eyebrows (variation)
,:-)	shaved left eyebrow
(8-{)}	sunglasses, mustache, beard
/8^{~	sunglasses, mustache, goatee
8*)	glasses and a half-mustache
:	fuzzy
:}	fuzzy with a fuzzy mustache
=:-)	funny hair
{(:-)	wearing a toupee

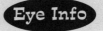

Eye Info

Smileys can have many kinds of eyes. Take a look at these:

.-)	one-eyed smiley
,-)	one-eyed smiley, winking
?-(	black eye
!-(	black eye (variation)
8-)	wide-eyed
%-)	cross-eyed
;-}	winking
@-)	rolling eyes
=)	long-lashed smiley
=8O	bug eyes
.)	keeping an eye out for you

Nose News

Did you not know there were numerous 'net noses?

:+(	punched in the nose
:/)	nose out of whack
:_)	nose sliding off face
:-~)	runny nose
(:+)	big nose
:>)	pointy nose
:)	no nose
:=)	two-nosed smiley
:>s	smelling spaghetti

:<)	turned-up nose
:<	stuck up
:n)	funny-looking nose
:u)	funny-looking nose (variation)
:v)	broken nose
:~}	itchy nose
:—:	two smileys, nose-to-nose

Mouthy Matters

Check out the mouths on these smileys:

:-$	mouth wired shut
:-v	talking
:-%	talking out of both sides of your mouth
:-8	talking out of both sides of your mouth (variation)
(:-D	blabbermouth
:-!	put foot in mouth
:-{}	heavy lipstick
:-(*)	about to barf

Tongue Talk

Take a look at these totally weird tongues:

:-W	forked tongue
:-P	sticking out tongue

.'r	sticking tongue out a little bit
:-f	sticking tongue out (variation)
:-d	sticking tongue out (variation)
>:-b	sticking tongue out (variation)
:-&	tongue-tied
:-J	tongue-in-cheek
;-^)	tongue-in-cheek (variation)
:-q	touching tongue to nose
:-a	touching tongue to nose (variation)
:-P~	licking

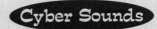
Cyber Sounds

Smileys can make noises, too, you know:

:-)	ha-ha
I-)	hee-hee
I-D	ho-ho
:->	hey-hey
:-(	boo-hoo
:-I	hmmm
8-O	omigod!
8-O —*	ow!
:-O	oops
8-]	wow, dude
:-o	uh-oh!
<:-O	eeek!
I-P	yuk

| :-( ) | ru-roh! |
| |-{ | good grief! |

Love Chat

Show your luv in cyber style:

[ ]	hug
{ }	hug (variation)
{{{friend's name}}}	add your friend's name to give him or her a cyber hug
:-x	here's a kiss
:-X	big wet kiss
:-*	kiss (variation)
:-	kissy face
:-*)	likes kisses
:-*O	kiss and tell
@>——>——	rose
(:-...	heartbroken

Cyber Characters

Your favorite characters are now smileys:

B-)	Batman
3 :-)	Bart Simpson
(_8-(I)	Homer Simpson
{ :-)	Marge Simpson
$-)	Richie Rich

#:o+=	Betty Boop
#:-o	Mr. Bill
(8-o	Mr. Bill (variation)
:-\	Popeye
\:o/	Gumby
7:-)	Fred Flintstone
(V)	Pacman
(-o-)	*Star Wars* Imperial Tie Fighter
/:-I	Spock
:————————)	Pinocchio
)	Cheshire Cat
*<:-)	Santa Claus
*<I:-)	Santa Claus (variation)
*<I:-))	Santa Claus (variation)
o-<:-{{{	Santa Claus (variation)
3:*>	Rudolph the Red-Nosed Reindeer
((I(	Robocop
>I(	Robocop (variation)
*:o)	Bozo the Clown
>:*)	Bozo the Clown (variation)
B-I	Joe Cool
EK(	Frankenstein
=):-)	Uncle Sam
=I:-=	Uncle Sam (variation)

Cyber Caricatures

Famous folks are flying around the phone lines:

4:-)	George Washington
=	:-)=	Abe Lincoln
:'}	Richard Nixon
7:^]	Ronald Reagan
5:-)	Elvis Presley
:-)==	Arnold Schwarzenegger
C	:-=	Charlie Chaplin
	:['	Groucho Marx
:$)	Donald Trump
:'O	Bob Hope

Cyber Friends

Meet these new friends. They're really smiley:

8:-)	little girl with bow in her hair
K:P	kid with a propeller beanie
d:-)	baseball player
C:#	football player
=:-H	football player (variation)
Q:-)	recent graduate
L:-)	recent graduate (variation)
d:-)>-o	tourist
=:-(	punk rocker
=:-#(	punk rocker with a mustache

{{-}}}	hippie
<{:-)}	clown
B-)	beach bum
8=:-)	chef
C=:-)	chef (variation)
8-)	swimmer
O-)	scuba diver
(:)-)	scuba diver (variation)
[:]	tiny robot
[: I]	big robot
->=:-)X	downtown dude
:-]	blockhead
o:-)-o	doctor with a stethoscope
8(:-)	Mousketeer
:?)	philosopher
:%)	accountant
<<<<(:-)	hat salesperson
<:I	dunce
<:-(	disappointed dunce
+<I I-)	knight
+<.'v	knight (variation)
-=#:-)	friendly guy
8 :-I	wizard
8 :-)	happy wizard
>:)	little devil
(-::-)	Siamese twins
(-: I :-)	Siamese twins with hair
<:-)<< I	astro-smiley in a space rocket

:-[	vampire
:-E	buck-toothed vampire
:-F	buck-toothed vampire with a tooth missing

Digital Animals

Arf, arf! Quack, quack! Gobble, gobble! That's what these E-animals are saying:

:3-<	dog
}:-<	cat
:>	baby bird
:V)	woodpecker
8^	chicken
<:>==	turkey
{:\/	duck
8)	frog
>:-<	goat
:@)	pig
:8)	pig (variation)
3:-o	cow
pp#	cow (variation)
pq`#'	bull
}:-(	bull (variation)
8:]	gorilla
:= |	baboon
:=8)	baboon (variation)
:<=	walrus

6\/)	elephant
OOOOO<	caterpillar
~~8}	snake
=====:}	snake (variation)
I)	salamander
:)	salamander (variation)
~O:	mouse
d8=	beaver wearing goggles and a baseball hat
B)	frog wearing sunglasses

Cyber Pets

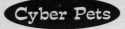

Want your own pet? Meet these kewl cyber creatures:

:]	Flurg, a pet smiley
:<	Flurg's little brother
:I	Flurg sleeping
3:]	happy cyber pet
3:[	grumpy cyber pet
3:o[	surprised cyber pet

Cyber Seasons

'Tis the season for cyber symbols:

~ O ~	summer
xXx—	fall
* * * * *	winter
<>~*~*~*~	spring

Side-view smileys are just as nice. They're just looking off to the right — and don't like to be left out.

.^v	basic sideways
,.'v	short hair
:-"	kissing
.'!	grim
.'""	pursing lips
.'J	smiling
.'T	keeping a straight face
.'U	yawning
.'V	shouting
.'Y	whistling
.'\	frowning
.'v	talking
8._.v	wearing sunglasses, talking on the phone
.\/	duck
.^v	pointy nose
*<.'v	wearing snowcap
@.'v	curly hair
=.'v	mohawk
:^{	mustache
:^{)>	beard
d.'v	hard hat
~'v	long bangs
!.'v	flat top

E-food

Smileys get hungry, too! Here's how you know:

oo>	ice cream cone (double scoop)
>>>>>:========	asparagus
:-'	chewing
8-P	reaction to school cafeteria food
8-*	just ate a hot pepper
:-*	just ate something sour
:-6	just ate something bitter
:-k	two lollipops in mouth

IHI: Internet Household Items

Why write out "television" when you can just write >[I

IHI	bookshelves
>[I	television
[*]~	computer
|——|	desk
h	chair
h——n	bed
~=	candle
-=	little candle
~==	big candle
o=	burning candle

Internet Eyewear

Four-eyed friends are fun, too!

::-)	wearing glasses
g-)	wearing funky glasses
(8-)	big-frame glasses
R-)	broken glasses
%-(	broken glasses (variation)
B-)	horn-rimmed glasses
8-)	sunglasses
B^)	horn-rimmed glasses on a pointy nose

Happy Headwear

You'll find some amazing things on top of smileys:

\:-)	French beret
d:-)	baseball cap
q:-)	wearing baseball cap backward
@:)	turban
8 :-I	wearing curlers
C:-)	headphones
[:-)	headphones (variation)
8=:-)	chef's hat
<:-I	dunce cap
K:P	beanie cap with propeller
*<:-)	Santa hat

B:-)	sunglasses on head
(:-)	bicycle helmet

Cyber Styles

Dress up your smileys in the latest fashions:

:->X==		tuxedo
:-)X	bow tie
:-)8	bow tie (variation)
:-)<>>>>>	necktie
*<8-)X	party dress
>< ><	argyle socks
:{}	lipstick
(: (=		ghost costume
&8=()	funny mask
B-)-[<	sunglasses and swimming trunks

'Net-cercise

Shape up in cyberspace:

O-G-<	walking
O-S-<	jogging
O-Z-<	running
o>-<	doing jumping jacks
	|(:-)	balancing books on head
O|-)	balancing an orange on head

There are lots of ways to say what you mean, and mean what you say:

M-),:X),:-M	see no evil, hear no evil, speak no evil
d :-o	hats off to your great idea
I :-O	I just saw the weirdest thing.
8	infinity
:^D	I like it!
:) :O :)	smile, oh, smile!
$-)	I just got my allowance.
:-()	I just stubbed my toe.
:-( )	I just banged my knee.
(:>-<	hands up!
:-$	Put your money where your mouth is.
2B I ^2B	Shakespearean message
:-)	comedy
:-(	tragedy

Dreamy Chat

When you wake up from your keyboard nap, fill in your friends:

I -(	had a bad dream
I -)	had a good dream
I -D	dream is coming true

Straight-on Emoticons

These are straight-on smileys. Some were created by
Japanese users and are called Japanese emoticons.
For these smileys you don't need to turn your head
sideways. Just look straight on and see what you see.
Right on!

^_^	smiley
^(^	smiley (variation)
^L^	smiley (variation)
\(^_^)/	smiley (with arms up in the air)
\(^o^)/	singing (with arms up in the air)
^)^ ^(^	two people talking
(-_-)	secret smile
^o^;>	Excuse me.
^^;	cold sweat
^o^	happy
*^o^*	exciting
(*^o^*)	exciting (variation)
@l@	You're kidding!
(@ @)	too many hours staring at computer
O-(==<	sleeping
O>—<	swimming
\o/	stretching
o/	raised hand
oo	binoculars
OO	headlights
oooo(0) (0)oooo	toes

.__.	frog
~M`'~	camel
>-^);>	fish
>—000>	fish (variation)
\(((((()))))/	bowl of chips
\~~~~~/	bowl of dip or salsa
oo—oo-Bo	semi-truck moving right
oF-oo—oo	Honk! semi-truck moving left
~~c_____	beach
^v^v^	mountains
/\	camping tent
==#==	railroad crossing

Mega Smileys

These are combination smileys and they tend to be very silly. Take a look at these crazy creatures — and then make up your own!

[8-{)	bearded smiley with glasses and headphones
(}-8]	left-handed bearded smiley with glasses and headphones
<*:oDX	clown with bow tie and dunce hat
d*:> *	fuzzy baby bird wearing a baseball cap
oo>8@)	pig wearing sunglasses with a double-scoop ice-cream cone on its head
8:= |X	baboon wearing curlers and a tuxedo

8= >;*{))	devilish chef, with a mustache and a double chin in a windstorm
8=}>;*{))	crazy, devilish chef with a mustache, a double chin, and a toupee in a windstorm
C=>8')	devilish chef with glasses and a dimple
}:^#})	bushy-mustached, pointy-nosed smiley with a double chin
(:)-) >-^);>	scuba diver watching a fish swim by
3:]<<<<(:-)	hat salesperson with a cyber pet on her head

Chapter Two

TLAs (THREE-LETTER ACRONYMS)

TLA stands for three-letter acronyms. The weird thing is that some TLAs are less than three letters and others are more. And some aren't acronyms at all. But WC? (who cares?) Basically they are nicknames for the long-winded terms that are a pain to keep retyping. Like BTW instead of "by the way." Using TLAs might seem strange at first, but B4YKI (before you know it) you'll be reading and writing them without even thinking. So if English DNC (does not compute) with your friends, try TLAs. Use these speedy abbreviations in chat rooms or in e-mail — they'll save you TOT (tons of time). Plus, they're WF (way fun)!

AAMOF	As a matter of fact
ADN	Any day now
AMN	Any minute now
AFAICT	As far as I can tell
AFAIK	As far as I know
AFK	Away from my keyboard
ASAP	As soon as possible
@	At
AYK	As you know

ATM	At the moment
B4	Before
B4YKI	Before you know it
BAK	Back at my keyboard
BB4N	Bye-bye for now
BBFN	Bye-bye for now (variation)
BBL	Be back later
BFF	Best friends forever
BFN	Bye for now
BCNU	Be seeing you
BD	Big deal
BIOYN	Blow it out your nose
BL	Belly laughing
BRB	Be right back
BSF	But seriously, folks
BTA	But then again
BTDT	Been there, done that
BTDTGTS	Been there, done that, got the T-shirt
BTHOOM	Beats the heck out of me
BTW	By the way
BW	Best wishes
BYKT	But you knew that
CB	Chat brat
CMIIW	Correct me if I'm wrong
CRAT	Can't remember a thing
CRTLA	Can't remember the three-letter acronym

C-P	Sleepy
C-T	City
CU	See you
CUNS	See you in school
CUL	See you later
CUL8ER	See you later (variation)
CYT	See you tomorrow
CYA	See ya
DIKU	Do I know you?
DARFC	Ducking and running for cover
DF	Dear friend
DIY	Do it yourself
DNC	Does not compute
DYJHIW	Don't you just hate it when . . .
EAK	Eating at keyboard
E123	Easy as one, two, three
EM?	Excuse me?
EZ	Easy
4	For
4-F-R N F-R	Forever and ever
F2F	Face to face
FAQ	Frequently asked questions
FF	Friends forever
FISH	First in, still here
FITB	Fill in the blank
FOAF	Friend of a friend
FOFL	Falling on floor laughing
FOC	Free of charge

FUD	Fear, uncertainty, and doubt
FWD	Forward
FWIW	For what it's worth
FYI	For your information
<G>	Grin
GG	Gotta go
GAL	Get a life
GD&R	Grinning, ducking, and running
GIGO	Garbage in, garbage out
GIWIST	Gee, I wish I'd said that
GR-8	Great
GMTA	Great minds think alike
GTRM	Going to read mail
HAGD	Have a great day
HAND	Have a nice day
HF	Hello, friend
HHOJ	Ha-ha, only joking
HHOS	Ha-ha, only being serious
HO	Hang on
HTH	Hope this helps
I 1-D-R	I wonder
IAC	In any case
IAE	In any event
IANAE	I am not an expert
IBRB	I'll be right back
IC	I see
ICBW	I could be wrong
I-D-L	Ideal

IDM	It doesn't matter
IDTS	I don't think so
IHAIM	I have another instant message
IIRC	If I recall correctly
ILU	I love you
IM	Instant message
IMHO	In my humble opinion
IMNSHO	In my not-so-humble opinion
IMO	In my opinion
IMS	I am sorry
IOW	In other words
IRL	In real life
ISDN	It still does nothing
ISTM	It seems to me
ISTR	I seem to remember
ISWYM	I see what you mean
ITRW	In the real world
IUM	If you must
IYSWIM	If you see what I mean
<J>	Joking
JAM	Just a minute
JK	Just kidding
KIR	Keep it real
KISS	Keep it simple, stupid
<L>	Laughing
L-8-R	Later
LD	Later, dude
LOL	Laughing out loud

LYLAB	Love you like a brother
LYLAS	Love you like a sister
MHOTY	My hat's off to you
MHBFY	My heart bleeds for you
MUBAR	Messed up beyond all recognition
NALOPKT	Not a lot of people know that
N2M	Not to mention
N-A-Y-L	In a while
NBD	No big deal
N-E-1	Anyone
NRN	No reply necessary
NTYMI	Now that you mention it
NUFF	Enough said
N-E-1 ER	Anyone here?
NW	No way!
14AA41	One for all and all for one
OIC	Oh, I see
OLL	On-line Love
OMG	Omigod!
OOTB	Out of the box
OTTOMH	Off the top of my head
OTOH	On the other hand
OTP	On the phone
OTT	Over the top
PDA	Public display of affection
PDQ	Pretty darn quick
PLS	Please
PMFJI	Pardon me for jumping in

POOF	Good-bye
PU	That stinks!
P-ZA	Pizza
RFC	Request for comment
ROFL	Rolling on the floor laughing
RSN	Real soon now
RTFAQ	Read the FAQ file
RTM	Read the manual
R-U-OK	Are you okay?
<S>	Smiling
SCNR	Sorry, could not resist
SFAIAA	So far as I am aware
SITD	Still in the dark
SMEM	Send me an e-mail
SNAFU	Situation normal, all flubbed up
STR-8	Straight
SYS	See you soon
2-NITE	Tonight
TAFN	That's all for now
TANSTAAFL	There ain't no such thing as a free lunch
TCB	The trouble came back!
TDM	Too darn many
TGIF	Thank God it's Friday
TIA	Thanks in advance
TIC	Tongue in cheek
TLK-2-U-L-8-R	Talk to you later
TTUL	Talk to you later (variation)

TTYL	Talk to you later (variation)
TTG	Time to go
TOT	Tons of time
TP	Team player
TTFN	Ta-ta for now
TVM	Thank you very much
TYVM	Thank you very much (variation)
TXS	Thanks
TWIMC	To whom it may concern
U-L	You will
U-R	You are
U-R W-S	You are wise
VBG	Very big grin
VR	Virtual reality
WB	Write back
WBS	Write back soon
WC	Who cares?
WF	Way fun
WFM	Works for me
WRT	With regard to
WTH	What the heck
WU?	What's up?
WUF?	Where are you from?
WWY?	Where were you?
WYSIWYG	What you see is what you get
WYCM?	Will you call me?
<Y>	Yawning
YCT	Your comment to

YKW?	You know what?
YHM	You have mail
W	Whatever
X-I-10	Exciting
XOXO	Hugs and kisses

Puzzling 'Puter Puzzles

See if you can figure out what these statements mean. (If you can't, the answers are at the back of the book.)

1. ATM I M AFK. SMEM, IBRB ASAP.

_____

_____

_____

2. UR GR8. WBS. HAGD, TTYL, ILU, BFF!

_____

_____

_____

3. HO. IHAIM. BBS.

_____

_____

_____

4. DIKU? HHOJ.

_____

_____

_____

5. WU? RUOK TLK2UL8R — F2F BFN.

_____

_____

_____

6. RU4 P-ZA 2-NITE? N-E-1 else? CU @ 7!

_____

_____

_____

Now see if you can write your own :-)

_____

_____

_____

_____

_____

_____

TEXT ART

Text Art or ASCII (pronounced "as-key") Art means pictures created by using letters, numbers, and punctuation. They are free of any fancy formatting such as bold or italics. Since every computer can open an ASCII file, this is smart art for e-mails. You probably see these pictures a lot. Here's an example of a popular one, a rose:

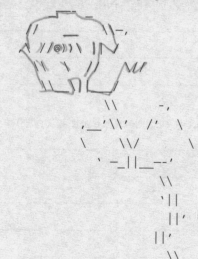

Here's another example. It's a guy looking over a ledge:

```
          \```/
       ' (o o)
  —————-oOo—(_)—oOo—————
```

**Here's a lovable
teddy bear:**

Moo-ve over, here comes a cow:

```
                    ( )
                   ( oo )
          /——-\/
         /  |    | |
       *    | |—| |
              ~~    ~~
```

```
        _.-.
      ,'/  //\
     /// // /)
     /// // //\
     /// // ///
    /// // ///
  (`: // ///
   `;`: ///
   / /:`:/
  / /  `'
 / /
(_/
```

Would you like some ice cream? Mmmmmm.

This butterfly's a beauty:

Electronic elephants are excellent:

Banana-o-rama!

Hey, surfer dude!

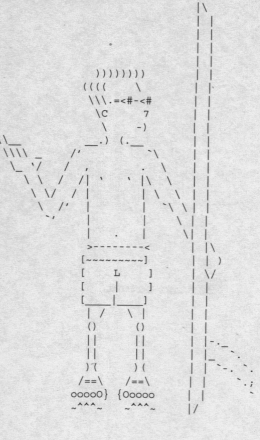

Wishing you the best with a birthday cake. Yum!

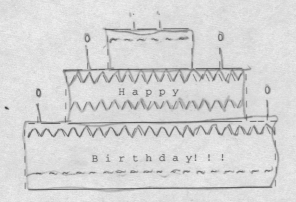

Have a heart:

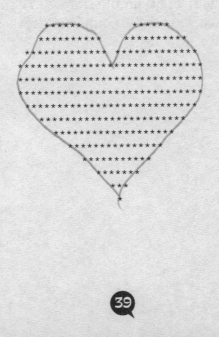

Peace out!

```
  ."".    .""..
  | |   / /
  | |  / /
  | | / /
  | |/  ;-._
  }  `-_/ / ;
  | /`) / /
  | / /_/\_/\
  |/ /    |
  ( ' \ `- |
   \   `. /
    |    |
    |    |
```

Can you create your own? It's easy. Look closely — the tools for text art are right at your fingertips. Just use the letters, numbers, and symbols (lot of periods and dashes) on your keyboard. And your imagination, too, of course. Begin with small simple shapes. Then as you get more comfortable you can try complex images. Remember, practice, practice, practice!

Chapter Four

ON-LINE JOKES

When you open your e-mail and laugh at a joke, you want to share it with someone else. With e-mail, sending a laugh is E123. Here are some funny e-mail stories that have been making people LOL.

Spell Checkers Poem

Eye halve a spelling chequer
It came with my pea sea
It plainly marques four my revue
Miss steaks eye kin knot sea.

Eye strike a key and type a word
And weight four it two say
Weather eye am wrong oar write
It shows me strait a weigh.

As soon as a mist ache is maid
It nose bee fore two long
And eye can put the error rite
Its rare lea ever wrong.

Eye have run this poem threw it
I am shore your pleased two no
Its letter perfect awl the weigh
My chequer tolled me sew.

41

Togetherness

A young man saw an elderly couple sitting down to lunch at McDonald's. He noticed that they had ordered one meal and an extra drink cup. He watched the gentleman carefully divide the hamburger in half, then count out the fries, one for him, one for her, until each had half. Then the old man poured half of the soft drink into the extra cup and set that in front of his wife. The old man then began to eat, and his wife sat watching. The young man decided to ask if they would allow him to purchase another meal for them so that they didn't have to split theirs. The old gentleman said, "Oh, no. We've been married fifty years, and everything has always been and will always be shared, fifty/fifty." The young man then asked the wife if she was going to eat, and she replied, "Not yet. It's his turn with the teeth."

English? It's A Crazy Language!

Let's face it — English is a crazy language.

There is no egg in eggplant or ham in hamburger. There is neither apple nor pine in pineapple.

English muffins weren't invented in England. French fries and French toast? Nope, not from France.

Quicksand can work slowly, boxing rings are square, and a guinea pig is neither from Guinea nor is it a pig.

And why is it that writers write but fingers don't fing, grocers don't groce, and hammers don't ham? If the plural of tooth is teeth, why isn't the plural of booth beeth?

One goose: two geese. One moose: two meese?

If you have a bunch of odds and ends and get rid of all but one of them, what do you call it?

If teachers taught, why didn't preachers praught? If vegetarians eat vegetables, what do humanitarians eat?

Isn't it weird that people recite at a play and play at a recital? Ship by truck and send cargo by ship? Have noses that run and feet that smell? Park on driveways and drive on parkways?

How can a slim chance and a fat chance be the same, while a wise man and a wise guy are opposites? How can overlook and oversee be opposite, while quite a few and quite a lot are alike?

And where are all those people who *are* spring chickens or who would *actually* hurt a fly?

Isn't it crazy that a house can burn up as it burns down? And you fill in a form by filling it out? And an alarm clock goes off by going on?

English was invented by people, not computers, and it reflects the creativity of the human race (which, of course, isn't a race at all). That is why, when the stars are out, they are visible, but when the lights are out, they are invisible. And why, when I wind up my watch, I start it, but when I wind up this essay, I end it.

The Thief

A man in Paris almost got away with stealing several paintings from an art museum. After plotting the crime, breaking into the museum, avoiding security, sneaking out, and escaping with the goods, he was captured only two blocks away when his van ran out of gas. When asked how he could mastermind such a crime and then make such an obvious error, he replied: "I had no Monet to buy Degas to make the Van Gogh."

Chapter Five

GAMES AND QUIZZES

Computer Geek Quiz

It's playtime! On-line quizzes are way more fun than the kind you just get in school. And games? Those are always fun :-)

Are you a computer geek? Take this quiz to find out.

1. I have moss growing:
   a) In my garden
   b) In my bathroom
   c) On my teeth

2. When I open my mouth at parties, people:
   a) Listen
   b) Ease away slowly
   c) Stuff a live weasel down my throat

3. I think computers are:
   a) Uninteresting
   b) Interesting
   c) Way too slow for the stuff I want to do

4. In general, people:
a) Like me
b) Don't like me
c) People? What people?

5. My friends are:
a) Diverse
b) People I know from school
c) Electronic machines, usually boxy in shape, that perform rapid, complex applications in addition to compiling and correlating tons of data

6. My dream vacation is:
a) Tibet
b) Europe
c) In a room with lots of fluorescent lights and an unlimited supply of soda

7. My job prospects are:
a) Abysmal
b) Adequate
c) They pay people to do this?

How did you rate? Are you a full-on computer geek? If you answered "c" to one or more questions, then you should probably try to spend a little more time outside (away from your computer) ;-)

Try out these exciting exercises that have been enter-taining — and stumping — on-line users everywhere.

Mind-reader

This mind game is sure to make you %-)

Do this . . . do this now, and do this carefully. . . . Pick a number between 1 and 10. Multiply that number by 9. Now, add all the digits of your answer together. Subtract 5 from that sum. Select the letter in the alphabet that corresponds to the number. That is, 1=A, 2=B, 3=C, 4=D, 5=E, etc. Think of a country in Europe that begins with that letter. Take the second letter in the name of the country and think of an animal (not a fish or bird) that begins with the same letter. Think of the color of that animal. Now scroll down (or turn the page).

[Print the following answer on next page]

Is it a . . . Gray Elephant in Denmark :-)

(Pretty weird, huh? Apparently, ninety percent of users usually choose that answer.)

Romance Predictions

Here's a quiz that claims to predict your love life. The person who sent this said her wish came true ten minutes after she read the mail.

First things first: Don't read ahead.

Second, get a pen and blank piece of paper.

Third, when you are asked to choose names, make sure they belong to people you actually know.

Fourth, go with your first instincts.

Fifth, scroll down one line at a time — don't read ahead or you'll ruin the fun!

1. First, write the numbers 1 through 11 in a column.
2. Then, beside numbers 1 and 2, write any two numbers you want.
3. Beside the 3 and 7, write down the names of members of the opposite sex. Don't look ahead or it won't turn out right!
4. Write anyone's name (like friends or family) in the fourth, fifth, and sixth spots.
5. Write down four song titles in 8, 9, 10, and 11.
6. Finally, make a wish.

And here is the key to the game:
1. This is your lucky number.
2. You must tell this number of people about this game.
3. This person is the one that you love.
4. This person is the one you like, but the relationship isn't working out.
5. You care most about this person.
6. This person is the one who knows you best.
7. This person is your lucky star.
8. This song matches with the person you wrote in number 3.
9. This song is for the person in 7.
10. This song tells you most about your mind.
11. This song tells you how you feel about life!

Send this to ten people within the hour you read this. If you do, your wish will come true.

Chapter Six

FRIENDSHIP STORIES

Since cyberspace is such a great place to keep up with friends, it's no surprise that there are tons of friendship stories, poems, and art being forwarded around the web.

Here's a lovable — and delicious — friendship "letter."

Hershey's Kiss

Roses are red,
Violets are blue,
A friend of yours
Is thinking of you.

```
              ,.-'Y _^-,
          ,.-'^H E ,-^ ^-,\
       ,.-'^ R S ,.-^        \ |
       \ H E ,.-^              k
       \,.-^                   i
                             Ss
                            kiss
                           kissk
                          isskiss
                        kisskisskis
                      skisskisskisski
                    sskisskisskisskisskiss
                  kisskisskisskisskisskisskis
                skisskisskisskisskisskisskisskiss
              kisskisskisskisskisskisskisskisskissk
            isskisskisskisskisskisskisskisskisskiss
          kisskisskisskisskisskisskisskisskisskiskis
        skisskisskisskisskisskisskisskisskisskiss
```

This is the start of a cyber "Hershey's" kiss-a-thon. Pass it along and kiss as many people as you can :-) (It is even okay to send it back to the person who sent it to you.) xoxox.

Bear Hug

You have just been hugged!
There's something in a simple hug
That always warms the heart;
It welcomes us back home
And makes it easier to part.
A hug's a way to share the joy
And sad times we go through,
Or just a way for friends to say
They like you 'cause you're you.
Hugs are meant for anyone
For whom we really care,
From your grandma to your neighbor,
Or a cuddly teddy bear.
A hug is an amazing thing —
It's just the perfect way
To show the love we're feeling
But can't find the words to say.
It's funny how a little hug
Makes everyone feel good;
In every place and language,
It's always understood.
And hugs don't need new equipment,
Special batteries or parts —
Just open up your arms
And open up your hearts.

Keep this hug going :-) Pass it on to your buddies :-)

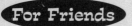

Moments

If I had my life to live over,
I would try to make more mistakes next time,
I would relax, I would lighten up
I would be sillier than I ever have been
I would take more things less seriously
I would be crazier
I would take more chances
I would take more trips
I would climb more mountains,
Swim more rivers,
And watch more sunsets
I would have more real problems
And very few imaginary ones

I have had my moments,
And if I had to do it over again,
I'd have more of them
In fact, I'd have nothing else
Just moments, one after another
Instead of living so many years ahead of each day

I would go places and do things
And travel lighter than I have
I would stand barefoot earlier in the spring,
And stay that way later in the fall
I would pick more daisies
I would ride on more merry-go-rounds
I would gather more clowns in my life
I would hug more people and hold more hands

I would meet you sooner and know you longer
And, I would love you better

Thank you, my friend, for being in my life.

Send this to everybody you care about; let them know
you are thinking about them. It will put a smile in their
day and a glow in their heart.

Friends Are Friends Forever

Take this time to thank all your friends. Remember those
people you know, like, and trust. People who know your
many sides — even the embarrassing ones. People who
did you favors. Those people you have fun with. People
who share their snack with you, who give you a friendly
" 'sup" or wave when they see you.

Send this out to those friends you just met this year in
school. Whether you're best friends or just acquaintances,
let them know that you're glad to have met them and that
you hope to continue being friends for many years to
come.

Send this to those friends with whom you've lost touch.
The ones you were friends with when you were younger
but now have grown apart from. Or friends that have
moved away or changed schools. Let them know that you
haven't forgotten them and that you appreciate their
friendship. Although people change and lives get
rearranged, friends are friends forever. And even if you
no longer have anything in common, you do share the
same memories.

Send this out to your closest friends, too. The ones you see every weekend. The ones who are like brothers and sisters to you. The ones who listen to you complain and who know your secrets. Those pals who would do anything for you. Send this to them just to let them know that you appreciate them being there for you and that you'll always be there for them.

Thank them and let them know you care. Friends are friends forever.

Send this back to the person who sends it to you and let them know you care, too :)

WHAT'S YOUR PERSONALITY?

E-mail is a great place to share stories. It's also a great place to learn about yourself!

Friendship Trees

Are you breezy, shady, or a friend to animals? Are you ambitious, lazy, or honest? Discover your tree personality. Find your tree sign (by your birthday) and learn a little about who you are. Then discover your friends' tree signs. It will help you see the forest from the trees.

Apple Tree, Loving
(December 23-January 1, June 25-July 4)

Often slight in build, Apple Trees are very charming, lovable, and attractive. They are also adventurous, sensitive, and sweet. Apples are generous people who live for today. They're also good at science. You'll find a carefree daydreamer with a super imagination in an Apple Tree.

Fir Tree, Mysterious
(January 2-11, July 5-14)

Fir Trees exhibit extraordinary taste, dignity, and talent. But watch out, Firs can be moody and stubborn, not to mention mysterious. Because they're reliable and likable, they also have many friends.

Elm Tree, Noble-minded
(January 12-24, July 15-25)

Elm trees are cheerful, honest, and practical. You'll also find them to be fashionable and forgiving. Elms make good leaders and often tend to make decisions for others. Noble-minded and generous, they are always good to share a laugh with.

Cypress Tree, Faithful
(January 25-February 3, July 26-August 4)

Don't mess with Cypress Trees. They're strong, adaptable, and faithful. Cypresses tend to be very creative with an optimistic attitude and a passion for life. They don't usually like to be alone.

Poplar Tree, Uncertain
(February 4-8, May 1-14, August 5-13)

Poplar Trees like to walk on the wild side. They're cool, courageous, and sometimes indecisive. Poplars enjoy fashion, pleasant surroundings, and take friendships seriously. With their artistic nature they tend to be disorganized, but nevertheless, they are extremely reliable.

Cedar Tree, Confident
(February 9-18, August 14-23)

Healthy, outgoing, self-confident, Cedar Trees are determined to put all their talents to good use. Quick decision-makers, they are often in leadership positions.

But be careful! Cedars can sometimes be condescending and impatient.

Pine Tree, Particular
(February 19-28, August 24-September 2)

Pine Trees love to be with friends, enjoy creature comforts. These trustworthy nature-types also happen to make very good friends. However, sometimes they give up a little too easily. They also have very distinct taste in things.

Weeping Willow Tree, Melancholy
(March 1-10, September 3-12)

Attractive, empathic dreamers, Weeping Willow Trees love to travel. Often restless, they are emotional but honest and true. Their strong intuition keeps them out of trouble.

Lime Tree, Doubting
(March 11-20, September 13-22)

Lime Trees keep themselves cool, calm, and collected. They dislike fighting and avoid stressful situations. They can be doubtful of others' unrealistic promises. But understanding the true value of friendship, these loyal Limes don't mind making sacrifices for their pals. Pay attention, though, they can sometimes be green with envy.

Hazelnut Tree, Extraordinary
(March 22-31, September 24-October 3)

Charming, undemanding, understanding, these sweet trees know how to make a good impression. Not afraid to stick up for what is right, Hazelnuts are tolerant and honest.

Rowan Tree, Sensitive (April 1-10, October 4-13)

Cheerful Rowan Trees have a deep love for life. Energetic and passionate, these talented trees are often artistic, sensitive, and independent.

Maple Tree, Independent of Mind
(April 11-20, October 14-23)

Imaginative and original, Maple Trees are often shy yet ambitious. These independent quick-learners are able to deal well when life gets a bit complicated.

Walnut Tree, Passionate
(April 21-30, October 24-November 11)

Full of contrasts, passionate Walnut Trees are known for their spontaneity and unlimited ambition. Often admired by others for their talents, they can sometimes be difficult.

Chestnut Tree, Honest
(May 15-24, November 12-21)

Chestnut Trees have a strong sense of justice and problem-solving. Vivacious and sensitive, they sometimes feel misunderstood. They are often very beautiful.

Ash Tree, Ambitious
(May 25-June 3, November 22-December 1)

Ambitious, intelligent, and impulsive, Ash Trees are hardworking, reliable, and yet, at the same time, very playful. You'll find these trees trustworthy and true.

Hornbeam Tree, Tasteful
(June 4-13, December 2-11)

Hornbeam Trees appreciate the finer things in life. With good taste and a love of life, they tend to be dreamy and highly creative, confident, but sometimes distrusting.

Fig Tree, Sensible
(June 14-23, December 12-21)

Strong and independent, Fig Trees have a great sense of humor. They also have a practical side and are very intelligent.

Oak Tree, Robust (March 21)

Courageous Oak Trees are extremely sensible and strong. They have both feet firmly planted on the ground.

Birch Tree, Inspiring (June 24)

Vivacious and elegant, these friendly trees are very approachable. Birches dislike excess and vulgarity. Their tolerant, calming, careful nature makes for a good friend.

Olive Tree, Wise (September 23)

Loving sun, warmth, and kindness, Olive Trees are balanced people. Their cheerful calm makes them sensitive to others. Often very sophisticated, these trees love to read.

Beech Tree, Creative (December 22)

Beech Trees have good taste, are well organized and very goal-oriented. They make good leaders. These imaginative types often make an effort to stay healthy and fit.

Take this test to learn a little about your life.

Subject: Horoscope
Write your answers down on a piece of paper. No cheating. Don't scroll down.

1. Name of a person of the opposite sex
2. Favorite color out of red, black, blue, green, and yellow
3. Your first initial
4. Your birth month
5. Do you like white or black better?
6. Name of person of the same sex
7. Favorite number
8. Do you like the ocean or the lake better?
9. Make a realistic wish
   1
   2
   3
   4
   5
   6
   7
   8
   9
   10
keep going . . .
go
go
go

go
go
go
go
go
go
go
STOP!

Here is the code to your answers!

1. Is the name of the person you are in love with, or soon will be in love with.

2. If you chose:

    Red: You are a very alert person and your life is full of love.

    Black: You are shy.

    Blue: You are mellow.

    Green: You are wild and wacky.

    Yellow: You are bright and cheery.

3. If your first initial is:

    A–K: You have a lot of love in your life. Many people admire you.

    L–R: You know how to have a good time. Your love life is about to take off.

    S–Z: You will be very successful later on in life.

4. If you were born in:

January–March: You will soon find a disappointment in matters of love, but the next season will bring a new romance for you.

April–June: Your love life will begin to bloom and will last for a long time.

July–September: You will fall in love many times this year.

October–December: Your current crush will blossom into a meaningful relationship.

5. If you chose:

Black: Your life will take a slight turn for the better and you will acquire some money.

White: You will soon develop a crush on someone.

6. This person is one of your true friends.

7. This number is how many days it will take for you and the person in #1 to get together.

8. If you chose:

Ocean: You have a wild side and you love to make new friends.

Lake: You are a mellow person and you like to keep to yourself.

9. Your wish will come true only if you send this to ten or more people.

Interact with Interactive Friendship E-mails

Here's an interactive e-mail chain. After reading the following list, users add on an item related to the topic and forward the list along to a friend. And so on and so on. It's like passing along a part of your personality.

Natural Highs

Falling in love.

Laughing so hard your face hurts.

A hot shower.

No lines at the Super Wal-Mart.

A special glance.

Getting mail.

Taking a drive on a pretty road.

Hearing your favorite song on the radio.

Lying in bed listening to the rain outside.

Hot towels out of the dryer.

Walking out of your last final.

Finding that the sweater you want is on sale.

A chocolate milk shake.

A long-distance phone call.

Getting invited to a dance.

A bubble bath.

Giggling.

A good conversation.

A care package.

The beach.

Finding a $20 bill in your coat from last winter.

Laughing for no reason at all.

Laughing at yourself.

Midnight phone calls that last for hours.

Running through a sprinkler.

Having someone tell you that you're beautiful.

Laughing at an inside joke.

Friends.

Falling in love for the first time.

Slumber parties.

Accidentally overhearing someone say something nice about you.

Waking up and realizing you still have a few hours left to sleep.

Your first kiss.

Being part of a team.

Making new friends or spending time with old ones.

Playing with a new puppy.

Late-night talks with a friend or family member.

Having someone play with your hair.

Sweet dreams.

Hot chocolate.

Road trips with friends.

Swinging on swings.

Watching a good movie cuddled up on a couch with someone you love.

Wrapping presents under the Christmas tree while eating cookies and drinking eggnog.

Song lyrics printed inside your new CD so you can sing along without feeling stupid.

Getting butterflies in your stomach every time you see that one person.

Making eye contact with a cute stranger.

Winning a really competitive game.

Making chocolate chip cookies!

Having your friends send you homemade cookies!

Spending time with close friends!
Running through the sprinkler with your friends.
Riding a bike downhill.
The feeling after running a few miles.
The feeling you get the first time you step onstage.
Being cuddled up in a sweatshirt outside daydreaming.
Taking a shower after a long run.
Forehead kisses.
Resting among the clouds on a mountaintop and bathing in a 32°F waterfall after a long hike.
Holding someone you love.
A long, strong hug from an old friend.
A spontaneous hug from a small child.
Long, hot bubble baths with the Sunday comics.
Hugging a grandparent.
Seeing a baby laugh.
A greeting from my dog when I walk in the door.
White fluffy socks.
Someone saying thank you.
A long talk with an old friend.
Having friends who understand you better than you understand yourself.
Laughing so hard that you cry.
Being friends with your family members.
The beach after the crowds have gone (around 4:00 P.M.).
Naps in the middle of the day.
Sunshine and stardust.
Catching a look from a cutie — and then meeting that person!
That time in the late afternoon of a cool, crisp, fall day when the sun is just about to set and everything is calm.
Hearing the words "I love you."

Finishing sentences for your best friend.
Knowing that for a split second you are the happiest person in the world.
An adoring look from your beloved pet.

Copy, paste, and add only one thing! Send it to a friend and e-mail a copy back to the person who sent it to you!

Chapter Eight

PACK-A-PUNCH STORIES

Some forwards pack an emotional punch. Here are some rather bittersweet e-mails:

Rose

Red roses were her favorites, her name was also Rose.
And every year her husband sent them, tied with pretty
  bows.
The year he died, the roses were delivered to her door.
The card said, "Be my Valentine," like all the years
  before.
Each year he sent her roses, and the note would always
  say,
"I love you even more this year than last year on this
  day.
My love for you will always grow, with every passing
  year."
She knew this was the last time that the roses would
  appear.
She thought, he ordered roses in advance before this
  day.
Her loving husband did not know that he would pass
  away.

He always liked to do things early, way before the time.
Then, if he got too busy, everything would work out
    fine.
She trimmed the stems and placed them in a very spe-
    cial vase.
Then sat the vase beside the portrait of his smiling face.
She would sit for hours in her husband's favorite chair.
While staring at his picture, and the roses sitting there.
A year went by, and it was hard to live without her
    mate.
With loneliness and solitude that had become her fate.
Then, the very hour, as on Valentine's before,
The doorbell rang, and there were roses, sitting by her
    door.
She brought the roses in, and then just looked at them
    in shock.
Then went to get the telephone to call the florist shop.
The owner answered, and she asked him to explain,
Why would someone do this to her, causing her such
    pain?
"I know your husband passed away, more than a year
    ago,"
The owner said, "I knew you'd call, and you would want
    to know.
The flowers you received today were paid for in
    advance.
Your husband always planned ahead, he left nothing to
    chance.
There is a standing order, that I have on file down here,
And he has paid, well in advance, you'll get them every
    year.

There also is another thing that I think you should
   know,
He wrote a special little card . . . he did this years ago.
Then, should ever I find out that he's no longer here,
That's the card . . . that should be sent, to you the fol-
   lowing year."
She thanked him and hung up the phone, her tears
   now flowing hard.
Her fingers shaking as she slowly reached to get the
   card.
Inside the card she saw that he had written her a note.
Then as she stared in total silence this is what he
   wrote . . .

"Hello, my love, I know it's been a year since I've been
   gone,
I hope it hasn't been too hard for you to overcome.
I know it must be lonely, and the pain is very real.
For if it was the other way, I know how I would feel.
The love we shared made everything so beautiful in life.
I loved you more than words can say, you were the per-
   fect wife.
You were my friend and lover, you fulfilled my every need.
I know it's only been a year, but please try not to grieve.
I want you to be happy, even when you shed your tears.
That is why the roses will be sent to you for years.
When you get these roses, think of all the happiness
That we had together, and how both of us were blessed.
I have always loved you and I know I always will.
But, my love, you must go on, you have some living still.
Please . . . try to find happiness, while living out your days.
I know it is not easy, but I hope you find some ways.

The roses will come every year, and they will only stop,
When your door's not answered, when the florist stops
   to knock.
He will come five times that day, in case you have gone
   out.
But after his last visit, he will know without a doubt,
To take the roses to the place, where I've instructed
   him,
And place the roses where we are, together once again."

Sometimes in life, you find a special friend;
Someone who changes your life just by being part of it.
Someone who makes you laugh until you can't stop;
Someone who makes you believe that there really is
   good in the world.
Someone who convinces you that there really is an
   unlocked door just waiting for you to open it.
This is Forever Friendship.

On page 70 is the sacred Red Rose. You must pass this rose on to at least five people within the hour of receiving it. After you do, make a wish. If you have passed it on, your wish will come true and love will come your way shortly. If not, your life will stay the same as it has always been. (No threats — just be nice and pass it on.)

The Window

Two men, both seriously ill, occupied the same hospital room. One man was allowed to sit up in his bed for an hour each afternoon to help drain the fluid from his lungs. His bed was next to the room's only window. The other man had to spend all his time flat on his back.

The men talked for hours on end. They spoke of their wives and families, their homes, their jobs, their involvement in the military service, where they had been on vacation.

And every afternoon when the man in the bed by the window could sit up, he would pass the time by describing to his roommate all the things he could see outside the window. The man in the other bed began to live for those one-hour periods where his world would be broadened and enlivened by all the activity and color of the world outside.

The window overlooked a park with a lovely lake. Ducks and swans played on the water while children sailed their model boats. Young lovers walked arm in arm amid flowers of every color of the rainbow. Grand old trees graced the landscape, and a fine view of the city skyline could be seen in the distance. As the man by the window described all this in exquisite detail, the man on the other side of the room would close his eyes and imagine the picturesque scene.

One warm afternoon the man by the window described a parade passing by. Although the other man couldn't hear the band — he could see it in his mind's eye as the gentleman by the window portrayed it with descriptive words.

Days and weeks passed. One morning, the day nurse arrived to bring water for their baths only to find the lifeless body of the man by the window, who had died peacefully in his sleep. She was saddened and called the hospital attendants to take the body away. As soon as it seemed appropriate, the other man asked if he could be moved next to the window. The nurse was happy to make the switch, and after making sure he was comfortable, she left him alone. Slowly, painfully, he propped himself up on one elbow to take his first look at the world outside. Finally, he would have the joy of seeing it for himself.

He strained to look out the window beside the bed. It faced a blank wall. The man asked the nurse what could have compelled his deceased roommate to have described such wonderful things outside this window.

The nurse responded that the man was blind and could not even see the wall. She said, "Perhaps he just wanted to encourage you."

There is tremendous happiness in making others happy, despite our own situations. Shared grief is half the sorrow, but happiness when shared, is doubled. If you want to feel rich, just count all of the things you have that money can't buy.

Today is a gift, that's why it is called "the present."

Time

To realize the value of one year:
Ask a student who has failed a final exam.
To realize the value of one month:
Ask a mother who has given birth to a premature baby.
To realize the value of one week:
Ask an editor of a weekly newspaper.
To realize the value of one hour:
Ask the lovers who are waiting to meet.
To realize the value of one minute:
Ask a person who has missed the train, bus, or plane.
To realize the value of one second:
Ask a person who has survived an accident.
To realize the value of one millisecond:
Ask the person who has won a silver medal in the Olympics.

Time waits for no one. Treasure every moment you have. You will treasure it even more when you can share it with someone special. The origin of this letter is unknown, but it brings good luck to everyone who passes it on. Do not keep this letter. Just forward it to five of your friends to whom you wish good luck. You will see that something good happens to you four days from today.

Chapter Nine

SAFETY

One of the best things about the internet is the freedom to surf and chat. But it's also important to be cyber-smart. Here are some important tips to keep in mind.

1. Follow netiquette rules on-line. For example, don't type in all capital letters — it means you're SCREAMING! Since you don't know for sure who you're talking to, it's best to be as polite as possible. That could be your mom you're chatting with!

2. Don't give out your name, password, mailing address, phone number, or school's name to strangers.

3. If a site asks you to register, first ask a parent if it is okay.

4. Don't buy anything on-line without first getting permission from a parent.

5. Don't be gross in chat rooms. (You may be asked to leave.)

6. If a message makes you feel uncomfortable, tell an adult immediately.

7. Never download a file unless you know who it is from. It could be a dangerous virus. A few viruses to be on the lookout for (and avoid) are a screen-saver called a Bug's Life ("BUGGLST.ZIP") that if downloaded will crash your computer and delete the files from your hard drive. Another is an attachment called the Happy 99

virus (Happy99.exe) that also crashes your computer. Be careful.

8. Don't believe everything you read. There are a lot of pranks and false promises being e-mailed around. If you're not sure whether something is real, ask an adult.

9. Stay patient. The World Wide Web is an amazing thing, but it is still young — and not quite perfect. Certain sites take a long time to download (some call it the World Wide Wait) while others won't load properly. Even your own computer might give you grief every now and then. Try to be patient. In the next few years, technology will continue to improve. So, for now, relax and try not to let these cyber quirks get you down.

10. Have fun.

GLOSSARY

Here are the definitions of all the weird, wonderful, and wacky web words.

Address
The unique identifier you need to access internet services. Another word for internet site addresses is URL.

AOL
AOL stands for America Online, a leading on-line service. AOL provides internet access plus member services, such as news, special-interest areas, and virtual chat rooms.

ASCII
(Pronounced "as-key.") ASCII files or "plain text format" files are text (letters, numbers, and punctuation) that are free of any special formatting such as bold, italics, or fancy formatting. Every computer can open an ASCII file, and almost every word-processing program can make and save ASCII files. The opposite of an ASCII file is a binary file.

Bandwidth
The term used to describe how much data you can stuff over a single connection in a given time. In technical terms, it's the difference (measured in Hertz) between the high and low frequencies of the connection. You don't usually hear the word *bandwidth* unless someone doesn't have enough of it.

Binary

Something with two parts. Computers use a binary language composed of ones and zeros to do things and talk to other computers. All your files, for instance, are kept in the computer as binary files and translated into words and pictures by the software.

Bit

Bit stands for "binary digit," the smallest unit of information a computer can recognize. A bit holds a single piece of information, either a one or a zero, on or off, yes or no.

Bookmark

Just like the cardboard ones you stick into a book, a bookmark is a placeholder to a particular URL, or web address. Bookmarks are typically used to record a site you want to return to, or one you like to visit regularly.

Browser

The generic term for software that lets you see web pages. You may use the Netscape Navigator browser or perhaps you use the Microsoft Internet Explorer or the America Online browser.

Byte

Bytes are most often used in describing file size and data storage. Byte refers to a string of eight bits that represents a single element of data.

Chat
On-line chat is just like chatting over pizza with your friends, except the participants may be anywhere in the world, and the words are typed instead of spoken. Chat takes place in real time and is popular on America Online and the web.

Cyberpunk
First introduced in science-fiction novels by William Gibson and Bruce Sterling in the late 1970s and early 1980s, cyberpunk is a lifestyle encompassing clothing, music, outlook, and technology. Basically, a computer user who thinks he or she is cool. Also: The name of the look associated with today's kewl computer geek.

Cyberspace
First used in William Gibson's novel *Neuronmancer* (Ace Books, 1994), it refers to the world you are in when you are on-line. It is the place where information lives.

Domain
The end part of an internet address that describes the file such as .com for commercial, .edu for education, .gov for government, .org for organization, and .mil for military sites.

Download
On-line, you can get software or files by downloading them. If you have software or files you wanted to send to another computer, the process is known as "uploading."

E-mail

Electronic mail is the digital means of transmitting messages via phone lines to other people's computers using an on-line service.

Emoticons

(*See* Smileys.)

FAQ

Frequently Asked Question. Also the name of the document that answers them. FAQs are all over the 'net especially in newsgroups where they're posted regularly and usually stored in archives. So, before asking your question, first check the FAQ.

File

A collection of data or program codes stored under a particular name. A file could comprise a letter you write to a friend, several letters, or a graphic image.

GIF

Most of the graphics you run across on the web will be in the GIF format. GIFs are file types that are readable by most graphics programs. GIF stands for Graphics Interchange Format.

Graphic

Any file that stores an electronic version of a picture. Graphic file types include .EPS, .GIF, .JPG, .PCX, and .TIF.

Hacker

A computer user who knows the technology backward and forward. Sometimes hackers save the day. Other times they use their expertise to illegally break into elaborate systems.

HTML

Stands for Hypertext Markup Language. HTML is the language used to create hypertext, which means it's the foundation of the web as we know it. HTML was used to create every single page you've ever visited on the web. HTML uses a series of commands to tell your browser how to display each page (such as size and style graphics) and create links.

Interactive

Any technology that allows the user to exchange information with a computer program, so that the user and the program "interact." This interaction can be as simple as clicking buttons or typing something in, or as complex as steering a car or navigating a virtual world.

Interface

What you see when you look at your monitor — the collection of words, pictures, buttons, menus, and other stuff that lets you do things.

Internet

A network of computers all over the world hooked up to one another so they can exchange information.

ISP

Internet Service Provider is a company that provides internet access to consumers. Your computer makes a local call to your ISP, which in turn connects to the internet through high-speed phone lines. Once connected, you exchange e-mail, surf the web, or perform any other internet activities.

JPEG

Like a GIF, JPEG is a graphics format.

Keyword

Specific words you use to search for something on the internet.

Link

The connections between hypertext pages. Every time you click on highlighted text to go to another page on the web, you're following a link.

Mail Server

The part of your ISP's server that handles incoming and outgoing mail.

Memory

The place where computers store all previous computations. Memory comes in two flavors, RAM and ROM.

Message Boards

(Sometimes called bulletin boards.) Places where you can read and reply to public messages or create your own topics. There are message boards on just about every imaginable subject. Sometimes they're the best place to find the latest information on a particular subject.

Menu
An on-screen list of options for using a program. Menus can "pop up" or "pull down."

Menu Bar
The strip of words along the top of your applications. Like "File" and "Edit," for example.

Modem
A modem connects your computer to your phone and lets your computer "talk" to other computers over the phone line.

Netiquette
On-line manners — short for "Network etiquette." An informal code of proper on-line conduct. For example, when replying to an e-mail, it's best to include the relevant parts of the original note. That way the receiver can understand exactly what you're responding to.

Network
Any connection of two or more computers made for the purpose of sharing resources such as information, software, or equipment.

Newsgroups
The internet's name for message boards.

On-line

Connected to another computer via phone line. When you log onto your ISP for internet access, you are on-line. When you log onto AOL, you are also on-line. A computer that is active on a network can also be said to be on-line. A printer can also be on-line, meaning it will accept data from its host computer.

On-line Service

Companies like America Online that offer internet access as well as their own proprietary content.

Page

Short for "web page" and refers to a single file residing in a larger web site. A home page, a search page, and an archive page are a few examples.

Page View

A "page view" is a term used by web sites and advertisers to designate how many times users visit their site — literally, how many times viewers "view the pages."

Password

The secret word that will let you and only you sign on to your ISP account, read your e-mail, or access a subscription-based web site. Passwords are usually paired with a user name that identifies you on the system. Keep this password secret. Mum's the word!

Pixel

The smallest part of your computer's display — the tiny dots that make up the images on your monitor.

Program

A computer program lets you perform a particular job. Microsoft Word, Netscape Navigator, and Netscape Communicator are all programs. Can also be used as a verb, as in "To program a computer."

RAM

Stands for Random Access Memory. RAM holds the information from any programs that the computer is working on at a given time.

ROM

Stands for Read-Only Memory. Holds the basic information that a computer needs to run. This information cannot be erased. The "ROM" in CD-ROM means the same thing: read-only memory, to distinguish these disks from tape and rewritable disks that the user can record over again.

Search Engine

A web site searchs the web. Search engines take the information and use it to create a searchable index of the 'net.

Server

A fancy name for a computer that's hooked up to a network. Servers send files across the network where your computer receives and interprets them.

Service Provider

(*See* Internet Service Provider.)

84

Site

A collection of web pages that form a comprehensive whole. A site may have many sections, each with many pages.

Smileys

(Also called Emoticons.) The name for all the little sideways faces — and other nonsmiling variations on the theme — that help users communicate in e-mail messages, chat rooms, and instant messages.

Software

Anything that is physical about a computer is hardware. Anything you can't touch — like programs and files — is "software."

Spam

Junk mail in the form of e-mail. Usually mass-mailings.

URL

Stands for Universal Resource Locator. The address of a web page.

Virus

A program that can hide anywhere a computer stores information: a floppy disk, hard disk, network, or various parts of memory, modems, and networks. It can do a lot of damage such as reformatting your hard disk (destroying all your data) or corrupting the activities of your operating system (making your system act as if it's gone crazy).

World Wide Web

The World Wide Web is the whole group of servers that (through HTML) present virtual, on-screen pages combining text, graphics, audio, and other file types — as well as links to other pages.

WYSIWYG

(Pronounced "whiz-zee-wig.") Stands for what you see is what you get. The ability of a program to display fonts and other document formatting exactly as they will look when printed.

Here's what Kidsilly and Friendlee were saying to each other at the beginning of this book:

Kidsilly: Hi, friend! (smiling)
Friendlee: Hi, what's up?
Kidsilly: Playing computer games. Way fun.
Friendlee: Cool.
Kidsilly: And you?
Friendlee: Eating ice cream.
Kidsilly: (licking lips) I'm eating asparagus.
Friendlee: (Barfing)
Kidsilly: Ha-ha, only joking.
Friendlee: Have you met :] (cyber creature)?
Kidsilly: As far as I know, no. What's his name?
Friendlee: Flurg. He's a friend of a friend's cyber pet.
Kidsilly: Oh, I see. (Grin.) Hi, Flurg! Where are you from?
Friendlee: He says he's from the World Wide Web.
Kidsilly: (laughing) Exciting!
Friendlee: OK, gotta go (too many hours staring at my computer).
Kidsilly: If you must. Now that you mention it, time to go for me too.
Friendlee: See you in school, face-to-face.
Kidsilly: Later, dude. See you, Flurg!
Friendlee: Keep it real.

Answers to Puzzling 'Puter Puzzles

1. At the moment I am away from my keyboard. Send me a message, I'll be right back as soon as possible.
2. You are great. Write back soon. Have a great day, talk to you later, I love you. Best friends forever!

3. Hang on. I have another instant message. Be back soon.

4. Do I know you? Ha-ha, only joking.

5. What's up? Are you okay? Talk to you later — face-to-face. Bye for now.

6. Are you for pizza tonight? Anyone else? See you at 7!